MW00526123

Additional Praise for House of Sound

"'It takes a lot to say I love you, I mean it / and mean it,' says the speaker in Matthew Daddona's rich and impactful debut, *House of Sound*. These poems articulate not just love as an act, but also absence, longing, and philosophies, all as a measure of life and its relevance. To stay or to go? This is the central question that haunts the speaker. And when one goes, is one ever really gone? These poems ring with questions: 'I want their wings. I want their answer.' In sound, memory, and the lack thereof. In life, love—and the lack thereof. This collection is an exciting example of language as meditation, mediation, and conciliation, as well as action. To write, to love, to understand, to contemplate—these are all verbs that require action and attention. Attend to the quiet yearning in these poems. 'Because a shadow / wants to leave you / but doesn't know how,' attend to the way these beautiful poems move through the body as heartsong, as a form of human touch."

> —Chelsea Dingman, author of *Through a Small Ghost* and *Thaw*

"Matthew Daddona's *House of Sound* takes the reader to a contemplative space that only the best poetry can. Daddona's dexterous command of language unfurls into stanzas of startling insight. His writing is crystalline, alternating between existential long shots and close-ups of moments so intimate and well-drawn they will break your heart. *House of Sound* is as smart as it is sensuous, as metaphysical as it is touching. I recommend this book to all the searchers out there."

> —Caroline Hagood, author of *Ways of Looking at a Woman* and *Having Maxine's Baby*

"*House of Sound* is an exploration on modern living - its conversational nature makes the reader feel like they are the characters, right in the story and world the speaker brings us into. The anxieties over existing, personal bonds and relationships, and existential dread are all too familiar, and they comfort us as we try to find ourselves nudging from darkness into light, from isolation to kinship."

    —Joanna C. Valente, author of *Marys of the Sea* and editor of *Yes, Poetry*

House of Sound

House of Sound

Poems by Matthew Daddona

Trail to Table Press
Eastsound, WA

Library of Congress Cataloguing-in-Publication Data available.

First Edition
Poetry
ISBN: 9780578711928

Cover Image: "No Play" by Randee Daddona
Cover Design by Jill Tomchin

Author Photo: Kathleen Dempsey

Trail to Table is an imprint of Wandering Aengus Press.
We are dedicated to publishing works to enrich lives and make the
world a better place.

Wandering Aengus Press
PO Box 334 Eastsound, WA 98245
trailtotable.net
wanderingaenguspress.com

Contents

For the ones we lost too soon, but especially
Kathi Dempsey and John and Minnie Daddona

Part One

House of Sound

HOUSE OF SOUND

Because a shadow
wants to leave you
        but doesn't know how—
it takes light
years to grow dark
        away from itself,
the way a body
runs its course.

My father at rest
before the day starts,
        before I see him walk
from his bedroom
into the kitchen
        it must be sad
to be him
and see this
        and never stop to wonder
if he's being followed
by someone
        or if it's clean, guileless
but then I see my mother
and she's carrying
        nothing in her hands
and it will not be like this
the rest of the day.

I call this part
shadow play
        I stare as if half-awake
and change something else
a film on the ceiling
        and soon
trees, sun gaps, spouts
and small banter
        excuse themselves
and this is real.

I want to say
        this is real.

If I watch my hands
long enough
        they become borrowed,
if we believe
that we are worth more
        then it must be true.
My father says pray
but what he means is
        cup your hands child,
watch the water rush
from shoal to bank and back
        and think of me.

And he is not dead.
He won't be for a long time.
        It's gratitude
that makes me think
about heaviness, so often
        when I hug him
the way he used to hug me
I think of flesh and bone,
        and blood,
and, if the saying is correct,
if it runs deep
        between the chambers
then I know the probable
awaits; it's a bit like
        rounding the corner
and seeing oneself
for a moment
        stacked next to
every moment, you say
today I'm going to collect
        the bones
and you stare
for as long as you can,
        you don't remember moving.

FROM MOM, WITH LOVE ON YOUR BIRTHDAY

Today when I looked in the mirror
and saw myself aging with you,
I thought Earth wouldn't be enough
to contain us both,
but there it is
turning its constant light on,
like the woman next door
who doesn't sleep
but lives in a period of wakefulness
that your father calls desire.
It is not at all like that woman
I tell him,
the way her axis is always shifting
from one place to the next,
you are almost dreaming her alive.
Sometimes it helps
that the light turns off.
Sometimes we should
wait for the moon
and be forced to choose
between night and day.
I want to make the moon my painting
and string it along for the ride,
this way
when I'm driving I'd have two moons
and one Earth.
You could call me on my one phone
and complain about the signal.
Have we ever been so close as now,
the fact that losing signal is possible?
The Earth has one set of solutions
for contact and the moon another.
Your father has a theory that the woman
never stops desiring,
that all the world's light would be spent
in her hands.

I show him a picture of you, Matthew,
where the moon bobs like a second head,
behind you the trees sift in repose,
plans lay weighted in your hands.
It's the heaviness that gets me.
Last night the woman never came home
and the light zapped at moths for hours.
It's the waiting, too.
I think I might shut it off,
if only to feel assured.
Do you feel okay? You are, right?
I know you have so many cards
and that every year is a birthday,
but here's another,
one more.

RECOVERING SPANISH TEACHER

In all those years having never really spoken it
except in classrooms and once, twice, in Spain
as a young woman trying to impress
her advisors, or of course
having spoken it in pleasantries
between friends—*muy bien gracias y tú*—
who don't speak Spanish
like she does but could, really,
she thinks of all those years
having never dreamed in Spanish either
and how those dreams would have played
out had she been able to talk
to those guys in a language
that would've been foreign
but that would have made them understand
the point, which is to say that not all language
is communicative because sometimes it sounds
nice to be lost in the melody of a senorita
but at least, too, she would have sounded new
to herself kind of like caught in the throes
of a body you know is ill-fitting but that you try
on for size and walk
around in for a while—
the way the boys she taught in her Spanish II class
had rolled their tongues to create the L
of *loca* before turning their attention to each other
while she had seen so many times these boys' faces
totally empty while spitting back the words on the necks
of the girls in front of them and the girls
not ever noticing—okay, fine, a few times—
the closeness of the breaths on the other side,
how sometimes she would hear one girl, Sam her name,
brag of how close she got to finding the right words
to say to *him* though it wasn't *her* who almost talked
it was that unconscious part of human nature
that arrives right before the nervous breaths stop
everything.
        I wanted to say that I had so much to say

she dreams but doesn't tell anyone, least of all
the man she has been tethered to, seemingly, ever since
The Inquisition, which is what she calls her heart
the days when light is low and bandaged
across the sky, when her heart is less a heart,
and he is after something other
than *this*—but what could this be—and since
she can't shake its name as if it were
a moment in time, an epoch,
an age that makes her forget her age,
she says nothing about it or the crimes
she's incurred during its frequent raids having lain
frog-bellied and spotted looking up at her man
showing no tears in his eyes or barely reflecting
her own. This heart,
this heart of mine—*mi amor, te amo*—
No I love myself more than you know,
and in a dream in which all her former students
have perfect accents and grammar and had gone
past perfectly searching for their missing English
she claws a little deeper into the classroom
trying to find her own as if it were ephemeral
and wind-backed and could be tied to a string
and sent away to live in Andalusia,
where in the summers everyone sleeps
with their windows open, just trying, she imagines
to hear a stranger say he was so close
he almost heard her words come apart.

WITH GRATITUDE

There's a good kind of selfish,
as in caring for yourself,
or when a person who knows you
sees you in a store
and says that you look well
and you smile, and in that moment
think about what a smile gives the other person:
recognition, kindness, a little love.
You think a smile is nothing more
than a set of strong teeth and that the jaw
is the exception to the rule.
Your boyfriend was once strong-jawed
and then all his teeth got out.
All of your friends have teeth
that expose their fears,
and there's never any time
to tell new jokes.
Here comes the punch line you say
and hear the marching on your heart,
and all the knock-knocking
tells you they've heard this one before.
It's not the joke though,
not the sounds lapsing your tongue,
but the thought of them going places.
Florida maybe, where the old
never laugh and the young
never grow old, and the sun only stops
for death, so close,
you'd get a tan just living.
The person who sees you there is a friend
and you wonder now how many times
she caught you standing
not noticing her. Beautiful, you think,
this standing and smiling at no one.

SNOW IN THE GARDEN

By now human touch
is worth more
than what we affix it to
but in the bath light
of the house next door
a man uses one hand
to steal his wife a blow
to her temple
and what then?

They took him out
through the garden
where he noted
it must have snowed
past bonsais to the gate
grating the pavement
which caused a chain
of events—fresh snow
the occasional bird

a warmness, my wife makes
tea when I get to thinking.

DYING AS A FORM OF ENTERTAINMENT

Mom taught me to laugh when days were
long, how to sow and reap
time or to clip
it like a winged creature.
And then later, when laughter was futile,
a birthday wish to a past life,
she told me to lie
in the face
of sadness and roll
in the dirt till my hands came clean.
This was hard,
the contradiction. A commercial
with healing
on mute. All those small-time actors
shedding diseases
then going out to swim
in staged water. Not unlike
a cartoon where the mouths
move too slow for words.
She said I would never understand
just by watching. Because one day
it's cancer and the next cartoons;
in one case it's death
and in the other a land
where nobody ever dies.

THE WHITE DOG

reminds us there are no favors
unpaid. Today a crow was eaten alive
by our Labrador and I thought
how feeble a symbol death.

My wife smiles crow's feet.
Our house was painted last week with a fog coat
and on its wings, black

snow. I regenerate like a worm
by separating from the body
and wake up only half-alive.

Last night I dreamt of ice cream cones
and fathomed a resolution.

I watched snow dissolve
on heels of impenetrable flowers.

These are only symbols of time.

In spring,
my wife collects the bones
while I dig the hole.

The sun paints patterns
across the grass, stretches them through the organs

of ghosts. The dog digs back a memory
but can't begin to fathom
when it's done.

LAST DAYS FOR CHARLIE

lie down dog lie
down land where dogs
roam divot to fence
sun-spotted
we have the same back
we are the same
man is an image in himself
a cage is a low place
to never feel home
the sequestered barks
pinched by his lungs
are cages for air
just barely lilting a voice
I can call and he won't answer
he might not even see straight

his burial ground
will soon be unearthed
each day he prances around
and I scold him
for getting dirty
as if consciousness is made
to be clean I clean him
the soap burns his eyes
this bathroom of silt and limestone
is what I have to remember
the scent is burdensome
if we hold onto it
I hold a thread of fur
so long it languishes
if I call it cat-like
he notices

something else returns a miracle
of paws if this is dying
it is vibrant
I call him and he comes
our backs are sinuous like ridges
something might be hiding there
I think counting backwards
might count back his age
but today is for hard truths
latency despite his energy
the toy that is lost and found
departs dramatically
the ground is wet and soft
and ripe for aging
when he goes
I'll be a bitter young man

A Lesson

When I found Charlie lying there,
I didn't know if it was strength
or weakness that made me scream.

I know this: Sound can make
a heart break like glass
and that there are two sounds
for every
one heart.

First the
scream and then
the breaking.

Part Two

Last Night, the Caterwaul

POEM FOR LEAVING
(For KB)

I

Is it the feeling you're 4,000 miles away
and have left the oven on?
Someone will notice

two-dozen red roses
awaiting their turn.
Trust the neighbor,
trust the neighbor's dog who bites
dandelion heads clean off.

II

I regret to inform you
ten more ferries will disembark today,
two dawdling trains will arrive,
the lighthouse will con the fish
that swim centrifugally to shore.

III

This is the body of a poem
as it deadman-floats
closer to its title,
centripetally,
without a purpose.

IV

More than to safeguard your books
I want to galvanize the long-winded passages
that flutter in your absence,
busier than Joyce winning at pinball.
I've never read Joyce.
I don't deserve a bed,
let alone a box of your books.

V

If anything, you have left
your window open,
not your oven on.

VI

On the day of your departure,
tourists came
dosed in August rain
to order coffee with explicit instructions.
Rain supplants the tears of a child
who watches a bug land in his cereal,
then leaves once the milk bowl
of time spoils forever.

VII

The packing is never done;
your neighbor searches for dandelions
his dog buried near marigolds.

VIII

Do you want a Siamese twin,
someone to ensure that nothing has happened?
To be tied at the neck, like stolen
souvenirs of each other's worlds?

Or do you want a distant relative,
someone to write the story
of the one who got away?

TYMBALS

The cordless phone is baseless.
It rings and I don't answer it.

I plan garden time instead. The phone
spreads its wings, or like a bulbous

plant, proves itself to the wind.
From out the trees,

cicadas lift like porch dust
and from where I sit

I might just forget
the sounds made

from their abdomens, the ribbed
membranes like offshoots

of the flowers. I've forgotten
these sounds all winter

but now they're back
and some tiny alarm

circles below like a harbinger.
Whenever the phone zings

I pretend the cicadas will answer
and play back a memory

a hundred times over. *No, I have not yet
unloved. No, I have tried*

to bring you back.
The cicadas pass a message

through the leaves,
their vowels

cocooning, then cooing
like Oms.

I want their wings.
I want their answer.

THREE PREMISES ABOVE PEMETIC MOUNTAIN

Below stippled
blue above
pines stretching invisible
fingers upward, ghosts
on a gust of whim
parade the mountain looking
for food   or sustenance.

There is more down there—
a dead-moth bath
a baby bird drinking
its wings headlong into night
and by extension America,
stifled under the sheer vanity
of salt.

Premise:
All things that have opposites are generated from their opposites

The electricity of a fishing rod
connects eels to the land;
I'm reminded of a ferryboat captain
who can't yet see the shore
says the ship has landed
safely there was no moral
as Monday hasn't a time and place,
Monday moves past us
becomes silent dawn
above dampest rock.

Premise:
Birth and Death are opposites

So says Plato, whose childhood
shadow scarred the rock face
he spent his life
constructing an allegory.

Ian moves a dead deer
to test for life.
The brush has many faces
but none as perfect as when
it undressed, asked us to wear
umbrage as a garment the rabbits
could chew

Ian, we're better off
playing dead.

Premise:
There are intermediate processes between Birth and Death

Then I know
the bugled bird
sounds like a passageway
through a slant of light
a peculiar genesis
of rock
embedded in the salt
of the earth
our bodies.

Girls toss petals from their petticoats
in Maine to decide the rate at which
memories cascade the mountain
and land in the river-bowl
of time.

RIPE ORDER

As a line
break in clay
forms the metrics
of mediocrity
waves return
a facing shore
waving from a sky
that mirrors them

Suppose a woman is truth
and truth a mirror
and our own amanuensis
writes *semi-*
ologic
instead of *semi-*
colon? The order
when broken

Rises like steeples steeped
in precision
as lichen likened
to ruin
requires a symbiotic
design between people
and things
to begin in time again

THE LANDSCAPERS

The cups ache a little in the cupboard
when the milk spoils miles from the saucer.

There is nothing worth saving, save for
everything that doesn't move. Today

nobody died, yet every object offers its condolences.
A door swung open falters like a field mouse crying,

the clock chimes a second too early
for the second time—my grandfather's clock—

The Grandfather Clock. The still-dead man who lives
inside has been calling all day to say

nothing important, just that the world is always
sorry only a little early like the lawnmower

weeping a prayer at 8 am. The landscapers
take to their machines, but we don't

hear them.

WALKERS

Last night the caterwaul
was caused by pigeons
the cats lay
in separate apartments
where I saw one
peek like a pin-up

Em walks into my poem
 (before it is a poem)
just as I'm nearing sleep
before the sun has risen
and scattered these pigeons
back to their cubby holes
but now their noises
are like loud guffaws
and soon Em will rest
her head on the pillow
she'll shudder at the sight
of what cannot be seen
two dozen pigeons
scream below the vertical
pane of the window

It's like that comic strip
I tell her I cannot remember
but then I do
later Miss Othmar in *Peanuts*
Linus' favorite teacher
squabbles an unintelligible
warble that sounds not
like pigeons
but an instrument
played to the unseen

My neighbors are loud too
Em says and I hear them
bat back and forth like brutes
which is where the poem
begins until she tells me
the softest part of the bed
is its center
matter can't occupy the same space
at the same time I write
another line this one
falls between the cracks
soon we'll fall lost to this
clamoring will be for a moment
a vehicle for morning
eggs and garlic and tea
steamed past the point of no return
once the tea goes
whirl we will get up
there's no fluttering here
there's only the fracture
of words
misplaced
unguided
ill-advised I write a line
that begins with

VERTICES

We're outside watching mosquitoes whisk the white sides of our faces. Imagine a place other than here, I say.

Liz and Kaye yawn.

Imagine the pool outside Nana's house.

Because we are here. Because my husband's family views birdwatching as a quaint, perplexing sign of mental illness. Because anywhere other than here could not be here. Which is why he hasn't come, my husband. So I bring the girls along and now they tell secrets to the grass, stopping only to confer with each other.

Their secrets, from what I can work out:

1. Mommy's wrong—that's not a house finch, that's a house wren!
2. Birds are stupid.
3. Some birds are cool, like the ones you'd think were planes.
4. I heard Daddy call Mom a bird once and then I heard her chirp at him.
5. Once he said, "Come back, come back."

Such words.

Look girls, a willet! A sandpiper! A white-tailed kite. Did I ever tell you about the time your father thought ostriches could fly? We were parked in the savannah, in a car, we were there, and your father says I'm carrying on too much, talking like an ostrich. I'll leave, I'll leave you here, I say.

So go, fly, he says. Fly like an ostrich.

That's when the savannah heat barrels in and I sob because I don't have wings and that one prick of a mosquito has been trying to tell me something all day.

TOURIST TRAP

My wife and I settled on the afternoon lawn. A group of Parisian men who were consumed with the girl next to us tossed a loaf of bread to rouse her. The smallest one kept saying *hair*. We knew this because he gestured at hers. *Hair*. But the girl wouldn't move. *Hair*. She sauntered off in a dream, just as the loaf knocked her backside.

And she didn't budge. Then a slender breeze made my wife writhe in the grass.

I said, Keep still. Here. Distract yourself, here, help me count the blades.

She laced them, linking her fingers, in the subtle way of self-restraint. And I thought: Would this look like love? To her, would it?

The girl spoke just as the oldest man prodded her again with the loaf. She looked sparkling and amused. This confounded me, so I spit grass between my teeth. The men caught sight and intrusive-like said, You know it could've been your wife we touched. The girl translated.

I cursed the grass and those birds for which life seems simple. And then kissed my wife's grass-stained fingers.

RITUAL

When you had a plan
I trailed with aplomb

I stalked business meetings
waiting for you to curtail out

At dinner,
I set places for two

The first trip we took
was out of this world

I thought The Hague was a place
where tourists learned the lay of the land

Sometimes I think gravity is only a word,
other times I seek its permanence

Would you dance if I asked you
and after doing so would you thank me?

I love this restaurant and I'm convinced
the waitress knows my name

How do you say *the world
waits for no one* in French?

How do you say it's time
to end?

TREMOR CORDIS

Stories dress themselves,
white lace and red shoes,
every curve of grass explored.
And what's more—as couldn't be
explained in words—
a stone pressed to lips
grazed my wife's thigh, skipped
down her waist
to abstraction.

It's where she has thrown it that counts.

Past the jagged fence,
a fanfare of reeds,
each a dancing heart,
receives it.
They yearn for attention,
each reed a memory
of one that came before

                                        and after

A sunset,
a story of a sunset.

But words cannot adopt the world,
won't stop
for a stone on a hill.

She remembers the night was "coarse,"
and the moon "cleaved yellow."

I can still go into those reeds.
I can find that stone
a hurl it backwards into infancy.

Part Three

Human Touch

TORRENTIAL X

If every action has an equal and opposite reaction,
how do I tell you I love you
and then will it away?
You fire back and we exist where we began.

Think of cannons in the dark.
If nobody is seen, nobody will fire.
If nobody acts, nothing will react.

THE PROSPECT OF FREE SPEECH

I keep phone numbers like knives
at a safe distance from me
so I can't call them on a whim
or chop them up
and rearrange them
into new numbers I imagine
they must feel the same
they hardly call these days
unless it's the loan agency
or Eloise who says she's only
three blocks away with my pills
and how glad I am to take them
I keep pills spread across my fingertips
like ancient stars because they never change
no matter how many I take at once
or choose to dislodge from my mouth
whenever I feel sick which is a way
of saying I always know who
will answer my call

A Visit to the ICU

On the way home from visiting you
I saw a family smelling flowers on the side of the road
and I pulled my car to the berm where,
in a sobering vision of serenity,
I let down the window and smelled them myself.

Any small feat doesn't qualify
another. Walking toward a sound
doesn't mean the sound walked closer.

I deny your pain
and also your hospital bills,
from which more pain is felt.

Distance is equilateral and dependent on the sun.

It takes a lot to say I love you, I mean it
and mean it.

The family that smelled flowers looked possessed,
the way they threw their young to the wind
like letting loose of change.
This is dangerous, I said aloud to no one.
My god, they can get killed out here.
What if what if what if
one of those flowers
somersaults into traffic?

I imagined stranger possibilities
not even involving the flowers.
As in the act of pulling their car to the side,
the father miscalculates his speed
and the whole caravan plows into the berm
where, by the way, I wouldn't be because
the family was unable to smell the flowers
and so I could not have stopped to watch them.

I pictured them earlier packing for the trip,
in such a rush they left Granny in the basement alone.
Suddenly every small feat qualified another.

What's the line we pass?
We pass, we pass through...

Nothing happened to the family.
Back at your bedside, I scoured obits for days.
I held vigil beneath the coffee table
for news that was none.

THE CHUTE

In its first year on Earth
a fawn over red berries
in thicket
blind to our pickaxes
and pocket change
requiring even some love

Pricked
on ears by brush
and fur straps
beating flax
from its tail
the fawn moves but not stealthily

Through the briar
obfuscating the course
of freedom
seeing the river
slide like a chute
gush next to the highway

Maybe it's a bead of faith
maybe it's a straight-eyed glance
at neighboring white-
tails that will set it off
will get the fawn
to realize its plight

It sees the chute
and trusting in gravity
sets its shoulders
against the wind
all nature
all history behind

This is about the highway
passing over the chute
the fawn cannot see
because it has believed
in sound
as progress

Walls of sound
spill like the river
when passing the barricade
the fawn thinks it hears engines
crawling at glacial speeds
to die by truck stops

While tonight
with attentive thoughts
I await news
that she has arrived
through sedge black wood
safely on the road

Not because I fear
not because I feel
I should fear
but because white-tails
have shown a similar curiosity
for sound

That should my wife
veer off the road
I assume she has hit
a patch of flax
melting tactile patterns
I may hear the fawn

Flow out of the chute
to dry in her headlights
unashamed as when newborn
It eyes her struggle
with the metal above
all reservations aside

But history will remember
the highway above the chute
and its fragile remnants
like the dust of fawn tracks
like the invariable motor tempo
like the regression of our fear

AFTER THE HOLIDAY

It would be wrong
to watch them
and say

it's only always beautiful
the first time

      that she wrapped him
in her arms and balanced
his head on her shoulder

as snow came down
where children played
in the long-gone field

      and held him there
and thought of summer
and shivered

They came back the next year too
looking tired and worn out
      you could look and see

      their lives
beating against logic
      his head
no longer resting there
      or that the snow
never came at all

      as if edited out

(Later, she would find
pictures of them that day
and recall how his smile—
not pictured—
seeped out)

But mostly
she had seemed chipped away at
turned in by the wind and
crestfallen

that when she returned
the next year
without him
part of her appeared
to have broken
precipitously

(you could see that too)

the part of her that hurt
the most
was the part that
needed time to heal

the part that knew because
there would be no healing

there would also be no time

EVEN HERE

paying for a coffee
on the row
blowing smoke
and dead flowers
from pockets
we empty change
instead and see
the bills fly
past our beaks
to the side of the boardwalk
where we lived once
and were happy

but this won't change
not ever
even with the strum
of sand against our jeans
even with tide
and its indivisible sadness
and the roofs sloping
in identical time
and the breeze
and its aftermath
set to perpetual nothingness
like the poorest souls
or dimes of your eyes

ON SECOND THOUGHT

I

There was crossfire,
dogs fled in droves,
shadows stood behind their effigies
though neither was alive
and no tears were discovered by the fountain

II

This is how I spend my days,
watching wind blow expression
from couples' faces,
as watching is an airborne effect, like waiting

III

Shadows followed the dogs back home,
crossfire was performed routinely, no guns,
effigies were iconic to say the least,
and I wrote through the afternoon
until my family rose like steam out of the basin

A Friend in Nogent-sur-Seine Is the Next Best Thing

A car that crashed through the guardrails
into the four-foot-deep river
didn't wake her or make her learn French
any faster now the birds will have their final
go around the swell in this way
the one silent cardinal trailing
the tree bark's dust won't seem

foreign   just

absent-minded   breathing

in leaves the way
one drinks in water
the way no one says
quelle tragédie
when the river is dragged

POEM FOR RETURNING
(For KB)

I

Were those decadent symbols,
as Mallarmé said, *fatal*
ennui? The mutes of America,
the stars, trees
ask of your devotion. In Nogent-sur-Seine
France; April 2011
the town's nuclear plant
rolls its eyes behind its head.
We need you,
Paris needs you
without an atom of doubt.

II

The former green yards of Orient Park
catechize the Fall of Man. In Greenport
Winter descended as a lunar moth,
an Orion?

III

In the span of nine months,
one letter. One bud burst
as ink poured forth
then burst again.

The letter C is a consonant of change
and until sea change,
won't change. Write:
I see, I see it now.
Then sing me revolution (in French plumage)!
Throw liberty into the bell(e).
I thought, but did not write,
how swiftly our motives disperse
they scatter like buds on the ground.

IV

To become love,
dress in idiom.
The kids gave you the name *Amerloque*
and loved to hear themselves say it.
Amorloque. Amor-ica.
These are the bastardized phrases,
speak them.

V

I am almost displaced
writing from my riverbed of the Charles.
I lift my sheets above its silk permutations
where it's known to be deep.

In a bar yesterday afternoon,
I noted how locals here are
impervious to sensitivity.

Time is killed in jest,
this couplet needs more

VI

time. This is the waiting game.
Old fog
changed to new rain.
In a cross-sectional diagram
of the *Cross Sound Ferry,*
location is a two-dimensional
etching. I am neither here nor there,
a tenor of the sea.
The ferry of bodies,
who rows and who receives?
Patience is steady, unruffled,
that seagull harbored in optimism,
Sure, shore.

Prospective light
informs perspective.
A wan February
brings heirs of malcontent to their knees;
they are premature children of Spring,
bastard germs of progress.
Mother country,
receive or spit them,
Caw, caw.

VII

The roof is aflutter.
Michael calls
Starlings, Darlings.
This summer we'll pitch a tent
as high as their perches
and wait for their aerial calls.
A bomb,
a buzz, a darling is returning.
Run ashore with news.
Spill the country in blue-
green tide. The current cleanses itself like a fawn
and keels over.

VIII

Solace is an art form
so long as it muses.
In the effluent passages, mental corridors,
tongue-in-cheek, what's the word for—
French bread.
It's how Rimbaud passed time.

In the end,
loneliness appends death,
lets down its vacant eyes
and stares out.
Goodnight world, you've been great.
That's all for me, it says.

An inner urge, soft as a canary, answers:
But we haven't even broken bread. And—
and there's still so much wine.

Gratitude

It's sometimes an exercise in futility to remember where poems—and by poems, I mean *these poems*—come from. Some were written as recent as January 2020, while some were the result of my puerile outlook at the start of my twenties. Either way, they are poems that I am proud of, and there are people to whom I owe a heft of gratitude in making them come to fruition.

I would first like to thank Mr. James Stahl, the affable face of Southold High School, for first encouraging my writing. Stahl, you taught me the invaluable lessons of dogged reporting, revision, and, most importantly, reading as a balm for the soul. Second, third, and fourth drafts are *always* worth it. And to Mrs. D., whose countless sit-and-chats in the school library fostered my ability to waste time doing the crossword puzzle and etch sentences on the back of math notes. Both were better options than algebra.

To Carrie Howland, who spent considerable time reading my poems, being my shepherd into the literary world, and introducing me to the inimitable founders of *Slice Magazine*, Maria Gagliano and Celia Johnson, who published my first poems in print. Additional thanks to the editors of the literary journals and websites who have championed my poetry and added me to their talented rosters: *The Adirondack Review, Anderbo, The Barely South Review,* Forklift, Ohio, *Gigantic, InDigest Magazine, Mad Swirl, The Nervous Breakdown, Slice Magazine, The Southampton Review, Tuesday; An Art Project,* and *Yes, Poetry.* And to literary journals of past and present that continue to take chances on burgeoning authors.

This collection, of course, would not be possible if not for Jill McCabe Johnson and the talented team at Wandering Aengus Press, including Susan Kim Campbell, Julie Riddle, Tina Schumann, and Ana Maria Spagna. Your acceptance of my work made me jump for joy, but your edits, attention to detail, and tender love and care made me believe, as Dorothy once said, that there's no place like home. Thanks for taking me in as one of your own. I'm also indebted to Matthew Lippman, Caroline Hagood, Chelsea Dingman, Alina Stefanescu, and Joanna C. Valente for providing top-notch praise for this collection. Jill Tomchin, you whipped up one heck of a cover design.

To the former Flashpoint NYC crew—Arthur, Brandon, Dolan, George, Laurie, Sarah, Sharon, Quintan—we may not have kept in touch over the years, but our countless performances throughout the city reinforced the idea of art as a vital subculture. I hope you're thriving wherever you are.

To my comrades—literary and otherwise—who have made living pure joy: John Trotta, you're the Pancho to my Lefty, and I wouldn't be a writer if not for your companionship and devil-may-care attitude. And to Nate Lanman, whose friendship and creative output inspired me to write poetry after a long hiatus. To Levy Messinetti, Ian Andrews, Rob Europe, Chris Lupo, Noah Ballard, Mike Figueroa, and Matt Maloney: friendship is an art, too, and you guys are the real New York School. To Emily Hunt Kivel, for our conversations at Clementine and literary partnership over the years. To Caroline Hagood, my friend and mentor: you've taught me to never give up and have rooted me on when I've needed it the most. To Matt Petronzio, who, with Caroline, helped me create a literary reading series that brings me boundless joy (whenever we aren't too tired to put it on; let's get the gang together soon). To Tim Wood, my first mentor and reader of my poems, who was kind enough to mask his dissatisfaction as constructive criticism. To Phil Budnick, Rob Cammiso, Jeff Kleinman, and the women of HIP Lit for the non-stop encouragement and much-needed drinks.

To my Brooklyn College peers, namely Jordan E. Franklin, Joseph Fritsch, Jesse Katz, Ed Kearns, Leigh Stein, and Ryan Skrabalak. Our sessions on the quad, with the light reflecting off our lined notebooks, made everything feel easy.

To my grandparents, who have waited a long time for my first completed book. I hope it was worth the wait. To the rest of my family, who have supported me without judgement. Especially to my loving parents, Randee and Lenny, who believed my fourth-grade teacher when she told them I'd become a writer. Thanks for never doubting that. And to my siblings, Kaitlin, Julia, Michael, and Olivia. Watching you grow has been a beautiful lesson in humility. To the dogs too, especially Charlie, who inspired two of the poems in this collection.

And to Katie Dempsey, who has loved me each and every day and has taught me that the struggling artist shtick is not as redeeming as the one that makes art feel enjoyable. Thank you for making my art come alive. But more importantly, thank you for making me come alive. I love you.

Acknowledgments

"House of Sound" originally appeared in *The Adirondack Review*

"From Mom, with Love on Your Birthday" originally appeared in *Yes, Poetry* under a different title

"Recovering Spanish Teacher" originally appeared in *The Nervous Breakdown*

"Snow in the Garden" originally appeared in *The Southampton Review*

"The White Dog" originally appeared in *Slice Magazine*

"Poem for Leaving" originally appeared in *InDigest Magazine*

"Three Premises above Pemetic Mountain" originally appeared in *Tuesday; An Art Project*

"The Landscapers" originally appeared in *Barely South Review*

"Vertices" and "Tourist Trap" originally appeared in *Gigantic*

"Tremor Cordis" originally appeared in *Slice Magazine*

"A Visit to the ICU" originally appeared in *Forklift, Ohio* under a different title

"On Second Thought" originally appeared in *Construction Magazine*

"A Friend in Nogent-sur-Seine Is the Next Best Thing" originally appeared in *Mad Swirl*

"Poem for Returning" originally appeared in *Yes, Poetry*

About the Author

Matthew Daddona is a writer and editor based in Brooklyn, New York. His fiction, poetry, and nonfiction have been published in *Outside, Fast Company*, Amtrak's *The National, Guernica, Tin House, Slice Magazine*, and other outlets. Matthew is the recipient of an Academy of American Poets Prize for poetry, and his piece "On Shaft Mining" was a runner-up in *The Blue Earth Review*'s flash fiction contest. Originally from the North Fork of Long Island, he is inspired by the sometimes-erratic, sometimes-blissful relationship between humans and their natural surroundings.

CPSIA information can be obtained
at www.ICGtesting.com
Printed in the USA
LVHW051930230820
663959LV00002B/531